AWM Capital

PAID

A Guide To Maximizing Your Bonus, Simplifying The Money Game, and Securing Your Future

Erik D. Averill, CFP®, CPWA®, CKA®
Brandon Averill, CFP®, CPWA®, CIPM®
Robert D. McConchie, CPA/PFS, CKA®

AWM Capital

ISBN: 9780692161203

WHY READ THIS BOOK?

We will teach you the proven path to move from amateur to pro on and off the field.

We want to help you win, which we define as:

1. Fulfilling your potential to become the best MLB player and;
2. Maximizing the financial opportunity that is a byproduct of achieving #1

As a player, your primary focus is to become the best player that you can be. There are only 780 players in the MLB at any given point in time, so it makes sense that your primary focus should be on the field.

If you achieve your aim, the byproduct of that success is significant wealth. When you become a professional athlete and are paid for the value you create, we want to help you maximize that opportunity because that will impact you, your future family, and future generations.

The challenge: Winning is not guaranteed.

History is littered with "can't miss" players who never made it and volumes of athletes experiencing financial ruin.

The good news is the results are largely in your control.

If you follow this playbook, hire the right team, and execute as the player, you will win.

WHY LISTEN TO US?

Players are told they need to think of themselves as a business and operate as the CEO. However, very few individuals in a player's close circles are business owners or CEOs. Most financial advisors and sports agents are employees of a company, so, unfortunately, it's a great sound bite, but players are rarely given the knowledge and skillset to become "business" professionals.

We are former professional athletes, business owners, investors and are responsible for helping our clients protect and maximize their entire net worth.

This gives us a unique lens.

1. We have personally walked the path you are headed down.

2. We understand the risks and responsibilities that come with ownership.

3. We evaluate companies daily as potential investments.

4. We have a fiduciary duty to our clients.

THIS IS OUR BUSINESS

- **2019 – 2021 MLB Draft Clients**
  - 14 1st Round draft picks
  - 2 1st Overall picks
  - 2x Highest paid after-tax
- **101 MLB Clients**
- **$1,400,000,000 Aggregate Client Net Worth**

PROFESSIONAL SPORTS IS A BUSINESS

Owners that include billionaires, private equity tycoons, wall street traders, and a legion of Ivy League grads make it crystal clear that this is all about money. It's not personal; it's business.

I hope you had a visceral response to that last statement and realize the truth that it's always personal because we are human. Players should not be reduced to numbers on a spreadsheet. They are husbands, sons, fathers, friends, and role models.

Athletes are frustrated and angered by being dehumanized, undervalued, and painted in the media as greedy. At the same time, most players are confused and ill-equipped with what to do.

Our goal is to empower players with the information and skills necessary to make **business decisions** in **their best interest.**

IT'S ALL ABOUT OWNERSHIP. ALL AROUND.

You have a choice: Own your career and wealth; or waste it.

As a player, you need to take ownership of your career both on **and** off the field.

You will never be taken seriously or, more importantly, maximize the full potential of your wealth when you have relinquished all responsibility.

You own the primary responsibility, which cannot be delegated; it is your job, not anyone else's.

You can be smarter and more responsible. You can take on that role of CEO.

The great news is that you have a lot of control. You choose the game you are playing (i.e., what you want to accomplish in life) the team (i.e., the advisors), and the performance (how well you follow through on the advice).

And the best owners reap the biggest rewards.

CONTENTS

AWM Capital

INTRODUCTION

What is the critical difference between an amateur player and a professional player?

Money.

As an amateur athlete, you are not paid to play, but as a professional athlete, you enter the world of a multi-billion-dollar business. You become both an employee of a company (team) and the owner of your own business.

Baseball is a game. Professional baseball is **a business.**

According to Forbes, revenue in Major League Baseball has risen each season outside of 2020 and set a record $10.7 billion in 2019.

Once you sign your draft contract, you are now an employee of a company that owns a Major League Baseball team. A company's primary purpose is to produce a profit for its owners.

We only must look to the recent 2021 – 2022 off-season when MLB owners instituted a lockout to understand how owners view players.

It is hard for some people to understand, but quite frankly, you are now responsible for thinking about your career from a business standpoint. You will be forced to make decisions that significantly impact your career and future life.

With the MLB Draft, there will be a company ("team") paying you millions of dollars. Therefore, it's essential to understand that the team is making a calculated investment in you, expecting that you will make the team more money down the road in the Major Leagues. This is simply the reality of how a team views you as a player.

THE MLB DRAFT: A TEAM'S BEST INVESTMENT

A 2019 study by FanGraphs determined that the first overall pick provides a team with an expected present value of $45.5 million.

In the 2021 draft, the Pittsburgh Pirates signed Henry Davis for $6.5 million.

The amateur draft provides teams with an incredible opportunity to invest in highly talented players at an extreme discount.

Many people believe the Houston Astros' 2017 World Series Championship can be attributed to rebuilding their organization through the draft. Starting with their three consecutive first overall picks that began with Carlos Correa (2012).

On the next page is FanGraphs estimate of the Present Value of each of the first thirty picks from the 2019 MLB Draft[1].

---

[1] To see the full chart visit https://blogs.fangraphs.com/an-update-on-how-to-value-draft-picks/

Pick	Present Value of Pick ($/M)
1	$45.5 M
2	$41.6 M
3	$38.2 M
4	$34.8 M
5	$31.9 M
6	$29.3 M
7	$27.4 M
8	$25.9 M
9	$24.5 M
10	$23.3 M
11	$22.2 M
12	$21.1 M
13	$20.2 M
14	$19.2 M
15	$18.4 M
16	$17.6 M
17	$16.8 M
18	$16.1 M
19	$15.4 M
20	$14.8 M
21	$14.1 M
22	$13.6 M
23	$13.0 M
24	$12.5 M
25	$12.0 M
26	$11.5 M

27	$11.1 M
28	$10.7 M
29	$10.3 M
30	$10.1 M

With the MLB Draft, the team has an opportunity to buy and control a projected superstar at a substantial discount. Teams understand how important this is, which is why analytics have made their way into the amateur ranks. **Teams are running models to determine a player's future expected value which dictates the amount of signing bonus (investment) they are willing to make.**

This information should help families understand that teams are not making emotional decisions but making calculated business decisions with each pick. When it comes time for an agent to negotiate with a team, the days of a player or an agent convincing a team to "overpay" what a team thinks a player is worth are over. The competent agents — the really good ones - will ensure that if a team values you for $5 million, you get all $5 million as a signing bonus. An early understanding of this is invaluable for a player and their family. Every year we see players who get hurt when they have unqualified representation and cannot extrapolate the player's actual value in the draft.

For the team, **it's not personal; it's a business decision.**

The hardest thing about the draft is that the draft rarely goes the way you expect. We joke around that there are only two happy players on draft day, the first pick in the draft because he likely had the highest signing bonus, and the last pick in the draft because he didn't think he would get drafted. There is a lot of uncertainty and emotion between those two picks. As players, we went through this uncertainty and emotion, and we still navigate these waters today as we walk through these emotions, decisions, and calculations with the players and families that we work with each year.

We encourage you as a family not to make the gut-wrenching mistake of waiting until draft day without preparation. You don't want to subject yourselves to the emotional back and forth of, "I should have been picked higher than this other shortstop or this other pitcher because I'm better than him. I'll sign if I'm the 15th versus the 17th or the 25th pick, etc." Instead, you should proactively start to educate yourself to understand and prepare for the decisions that will be made surrounding the MLB Draft.

For a family and player, it should also be a business decision.

1

BASEBALL IS A BUSINESS

YOU ARE RUNNING A BUSINESS, TODAY

I want you to think about the decisions you and your family have made over the past few years regarding your baseball career. There is a high probability your family has invested money to help you develop as a player. This could have been in the form of hiring a strength coach, hiring a hitting or pitching coach, and paying for you to attend showcases or tournaments. This use of money has helped you become so valuable that a college is willing to pay for your education, and now teams are contemplating paying you millions.

For most of us, we can't remember when there was an intentional shift from simply playing the game out of passion to now dedicating our lives to fulfilling a dream of becoming one of the best players in the world. But now, there are scouts that fill the stands, agents fighting for your business, and websites that are ranking you against your friends and projecting as if they know how your entire career is going to play out.

It seems that everyone around you knows that this is a multi-billion-dollar business and has set up their lives to profit from it. Yet the one central piece of the puzzle - you, the player - is being told to not worry about money or the business and just stay focused on the game.

UNDERSTANDING YOUR BUSINESS

Service

Your skillset and performance on the field help teams win games. More wins result in more fans buying tickets, making the playoffs, and generating lucrative media deals for teams. The industry has attempted to quantify a professional player's value in a cumulative stat known as Wins Above Replacement (WAR). During the MLB regular season, one WAR is valued between 4 million and 5 million dollars. During the draft process, front offices attempt to project how valuable you will be as a major league player. **They are not paying you a signing bonus based on who you are today but on who you will become.**

Product

Name, Image & Likeness (NIL). As you most likely are aware from the recent NCAA ruling, you have the potential opportunity to partner with companies that will pay you because of your brand and influence. Depending on where you are drafted, this can range from thousands to millions. Trading cards, memorabilia, equipment, and supplements are categories companies will evaluate if you would be a great partner.

Revenue

The combination of your service and product is what drives your value, what you are worth. **I want to reiterate that YOU are the one who creates the value.** This value you have created will be converted into revenue (income) through signing contracts.

Typically, one of the first business decisions you will make regarding a potential career as a professional baseball player is to hire a sports agent. The primary role of a sports agent is to help you understand how the industry, both the teams and companies, values you.

Hiring an agent is necessary because the teams and companies have an incentive to pay you the least amount of money possible, increasing their profitability. An agent's job is to understand the value you have created and make sure that any contract you enter into reflects that value as closely as possible.

Expenses

Hiring an agent will also be your first significant expense. Agencies typically charge 5% on the gross value of a contract negotiated between you and a team. In addition, agencies charge between 10% and 20% of the gross contract value for all contracts that fall under the category of marketing.

For example, for every $1 million of a signing bonus, you will pay $50,000 to an agent. This is why we encourage players and families to invest the appropriate amount of time and resources in identifying the agencies with the deepest expertise and record of success. Too often, players choose agents because they like them, not because they know they are the best experts.

This is a business decision. You don't pay people to be your friend.

Sadly, it's a costly mistake as you risk signing for less than you are worth and incurring a fee that is not justified.

In addition to your agent fee, you will also have ongoing training, nutrition, and living expenses.

The Result

Revenue - Expenses = Profit

Money in your pocket.

Once you start to view professional baseball and the draft through this lens, it becomes evident that **this is a financial decision.**

According to Major League Baseball, in the 2021 MLB Draft, the 30 clubs spent $264,838,490 on bonuses. With 312 total picks among the top 10 rounds, the 2021 class signed at a 99% rate in that range, which is consistent with previous years. Only three players in the top 10 rounds did not sign.

WHAT ARE YOUR ODDS OF MAKING IT?

1st round picks played in the MLB

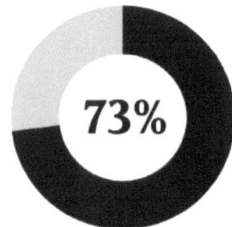

73%

Being a first-round pick is more than just preparing for your signing bonus. The odds point in your favor that you will also be a major leaguer. In 2021, the average MLB salary was $4.17 million.

THE BEST ARE REWARDED

1st round picks in the MLB career earnings

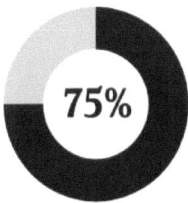

75%

have earned
$10 million

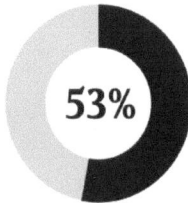

53%

have earned
$25 million

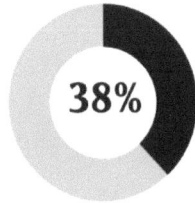

38%

have earned
>$50 million

AMERICA'S WEALTHIEST INDIVIDUALS

With one announcement from the podium, players will move from asking their parents for lunch money to becoming one of America's wealthiest. A recent CNN study revealed the following:

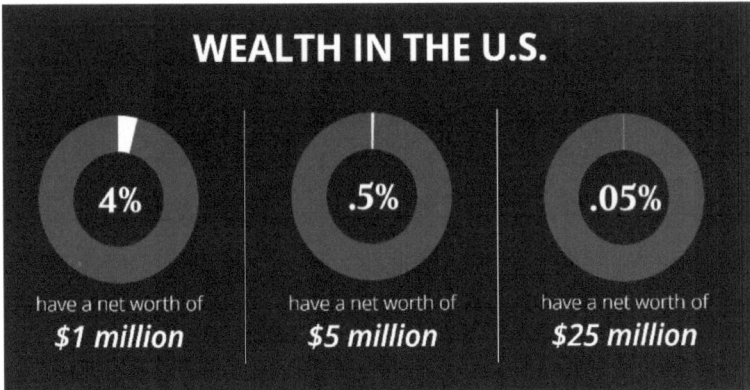

WEALTH IN THE U.S.

4%
have a net worth of
$1 million

.5%
have a net worth of
$5 million

.05%
have a net worth of
$25 million

You have an incredible opportunity to set yourself up for life through the draft. However, with opportunities come complexities, and despite being young and inexperienced, you must make decisions that will impact the rest of your life.

Are you prepared for the result? It is coming regardless.

We find it ironic that the entire year leading up to the draft, the general sentiment from players, families, and agents is that they don't want to talk about money. Yet, everything that is being done will result in a financial outcome.

After reading this, your first response may be, "We don't want to put the cart before the horse," or your agent might tell you, "You don't need to worry about that until after the draft."

As former players, we thought the same way, and we also understand and agree that your primary focus must remain on the field. However, becoming a professional athlete requires you to make intelligent **business decisions**. By choosing to be proactive today, you minimize the risk of being forced into making quick and emotional decisions that carry with them real financial consequences.

The most harmful and inaccurate advice that many players receive before the draft is, "You don't need a financial team before the draft." This line of thinking is naïve and dangerous because financial advice has been reduced to investments.

It is true that you don't have any money to invest *today,* so it is not investments that need to be discussed in the context of financial advice. Instead of investments, it is the preparation that helps you understand that you are making the most significant financial decision of your life. Financial advice you should be actively thinking about includes:

- The net-present value of your college education.
- The net signing bonus you receive **after** taxes.
- Whether residency will impact the amount of signing bonus money that actually ends up in my bank account.
- What does this money represent to me personally, as my goals and priorities are personal to me and my circumstances?

If you have an agent telling you not to worry about the financial side until after the draft, you should probably look for new representation.

We understand that this is a bold statement, but if their advice is to make the most significant financial decision of your life without financial experts, how trustworthy are they, and are they giving you advice outside of their expertise?

Being prepared is not counting your chickens before they hatch. It's putting you and your family in the best position to enjoy the draft process and putting you and your family in the best possible position to succeed and make the right decision.

2

WHAT'S YOUR NUMBER?

Should you sign a professional contract or head to campus?

Whether going to college for the first time or going back to school, it will be you and your agent's job to determine how teams value you and compare that against the number you have set to forgo your college education. The decision on whether to begin a professional baseball career is likely one of the most significant determining factors of the trajectory of your life moving forward.

How prepared and confident are you that you would make the right decision?

Many factors should be considered when deciding to sign a professional contract. However, for most players, it's a question of money.

The industry is asking: "What's Your Number?"

The reality is that everyone has a different "number," and there is a lot of work that should go into discovering what your number should be.

So, how much is enough?

THIS IS A FINANCIAL DECISION

For many families, their number is just a nice, big round number — whether it's one million, two million, or three million, or more — but it's not really based specifically on any sort of valuation that's calculated on the college education or the present value of the future earnings associated with the degree. We will have some variation of a number, but rarely has there been an analysis of how that money after-tax will impact their lives.

You will also get a different answer depending on who you ask. The answer is often largely influenced by their incentives. If you asked the college coach, they would have a slightly higher number than the local scout. That's not to be taken as one is right or wrong, but it's important to know what is biased versus unbiased advice.

This is where the rubber meets the road, and this is most definitely a financial decision.

We encourage your family to take the time to process that as a player, you are about to say yes or no to a decision that will change the trajectory of your life, and it better be something that you have put a lot of work into. Not just because somebody told you two million dollars wasn't enough money.

The first step for you and your family should be to discuss your best interests now and in the future. **Specifically, what amount of money after-tax will it take for you to forgo or delay college completion and begin your professional career?**

WHAT IS THE NET-PRESENT VALUE OF YOUR COLLEGE DEGREE?

It is universally understood that a college education is extremely valuable. Studies show that individuals with a bachelor's degree are projected to make an average of $1 million more in their lifetimes than those without one. There is an actual financial cost and risk associated with foregoing or delaying college. On top of the risks is that data strongly suggests that only a small percentage of MLB Draft Picks utilize the College Education Plan included as part of their initial contract.

However, I think we would all agree that not all college educations are equal in value.

Vanderbilt is easy to talk about because Tim Corbin has built an absolute machine. The academic institution is hands down an elite educational institution. However, the earning capacity if you graduate from Vanderbilt as pre-law and then go to law school versus someone who shows up on campus doing the bare minimum solely focused on getting to the next draft is vastly different.

So first and foremost, what is the **net present value** of your college degree?

What I mean by "net-present value" is: if you graduate from Vanderbilt and enter the workforce at 22 years old, add up all of your years of earnings and then bring that back to today using a fancy term called a "discount rate." What is the value of that in today's dollars?

That's the first calculation.

Next, you have to factor in if attending college will cost anything, or are you on a 100 percent scholarship? Unfortunately, due to the limitations on NCAA scholarships available to college baseball programs, most players are not on 100% scholarship. We have worked with a client who was a top 10 overall pick, played at a big-time school, and had over $20,000 in student loans. This was a high-profile guy out of high school, so there may be an actual cost to go to college.

You can do this calculation to help you figure out what your degree is worth, but **you are not done yet.**

WHAT IS THE NET-PRESENT VALUE OF YOUR SIGNING BONUS, MLB COLLEGE SCHOLARSHIP PLAN, AND POTENTIAL FUTURE EARNINGS?

If you sign a professional contract, it is not just the dollar amount of the signing bonus that you will be receiving. You will most likely receive the MLB College Education Plan, which pays 100% of your tuition. However, unlike a scholarship from the university, the MLB money is taxed.

It's not what you sign for but what you keep that is the important number. The next step is to calculate the net (after-tax) amount of the combined value of your signing bonus and college scholarship plan.

Do you live in Florida? Do you live in California? Are you drafted by a team that has Spring Training in Florida? Or are you drafted by a team that has Spring Training in Arizona? When you sign, are they sending you to the New York Penn league or Gulf Coast League?

In future chapters, we will get more into how your signing bonus is taxed, but once again, the conversation goes back to a financial calculation that every family must do.

Your agent will be a valuable resource through this process, but after reading this, I encourage you to call them and ask, "Can you run a net present value calculation for me?" Unfortunately, most of them will answer, "I'm not a financial expert."

This is not meant to diminish the agent's value. The good ones deservedly earn their commission. It is to help reframe your decision and make sure you understand the importance of having tax and financial experts on your team before the draft.

What is the value of starting your professional career today?

Once again, it depends.

If your son is Mike Trout or Bo Bichette, there is enormous value in playing professional baseball as soon as possible. In 2012, Trout earned $480,000 on his way to winning the Rookie of the Year. At the same time, his fellow 2009 high school graduates and draft peers who decided to attend a four-year college were completing their junior year of school. However, statistically speaking, Trout and Bichette are the exceptions and not the rule.

If you recall the stats from the previous chapter that most draft players will not have a significant MLB career, it's clear that the value of a college degree cannot be understated.

MAKING A BUSINESS DECISION

Would you agree that if someone offered you a sum of money today that outweighs the *potential* expected value of the earnings you would receive from your college degree, you might want to consider it?

Now add in the prospect of playing professional baseball along with the opportunity to earn multi-generational wealth, and this becomes a lot more enticing.

The Intangible

The items discussed above are tangible ways to determine "Your Number," but many intangible factors also come into play. One of the most important questions to ask is, am I ready for professional baseball? If you are a top prospect, you are most likely prepared for the physicality of professional baseball, but are you ready for the mental side of the game? Are you ready to be on the road for more than half of the year? Are you prepared to live on a minor league salary - as little as $6,600 per year? These are all questions that we faced when we signed professional contracts, and we could come up with many more.

QUESTIONS TO ASK YOURSELF

- If I sign a professional contract today, is it realistic that I will return to college later to earn a degree?

- What amount of money will allow me to pursue my degree later in life, assuming that the cost of education is higher 5-10 years in the future?

- If I have a family when my career is over, will the amount of money in the college scholarship plan cover the living expenses for my family and me?

- If I was not a professional baseball player, what career field would I pursue? Does that career require a college degree?

- Am I emotionally ready for a career in professional baseball, or would a college atmosphere be better for me at this time?

- How close am I to being ready to play in the Major Leagues?

FREEDOM TO FOCUS ON PLAYING

A lot of what we hear from families as to why they don't go through this process includes:

- We don't want to count our chickens before they hatch.

- We don't want our son to be distracted from having to perform on the field.

While understandable, the focus is also misplaced by too many people that do not understand the importance of the financial preparation that goes into the decision-making process. Educating yourself on the financial side and preparing for the Draft and what it presents removes a lot of the stress and distractions that pull you away from what you need to be doing.

You can stop worrying about what articles are saying or your ranking on Perfect Game or X, Y, Z, and go out and get to work and get better.

You can have genuine confidence by understanding how teams value you as a player and gain clarity on the value of your college education.

And the best thing you can do to increase your opportunity is get better at your skillset, baseball.

3

HOW YOUR BONUS IS TAXED

How are MLB Draft signing bonuses taxed?

As an athlete, you should consider that question long before draft day. There are many factors to consider when deciding if you will remain an amateur player or start your professional career. For most players, it comes down to money.

Yet, players and their families are rarely proactive in understanding how to maximize the **after-tax** amount of a signing bonus.

Before you sign your first contract, you have a unique opportunity to take ownership of your wealth from day one. This is a financial decision. Seek out the expertise of a financial team, preferably a family office that works with professional athletes, to avoid costly mistakes that new players often make in negotiating a signing bonus.

Sure, taxes may seem like a boring subject. But if discussing this topic puts more money in your pocket, that's time well spent.

In the 2021 MLB Draft, we worked with an agent to negotiate a player's signing bonus structure, resulting in the player receiving an extra $700,000 after-tax.

But that doesn't always happen.

DON'T RELY ON YOUR AGENT FOR TAX PLANNING

Traditionally, a player will hire a sports agent who is a critical member of your advisory team. Your agent exists to ensure that you receive the money you are due.

Step 1: Through your performance, you create value for which a team is willing to pay.

Step 2: Your agent negotiates with the team to get you paid for your total value.

Which results in what? Money.

Your agent's main priority is negotiating the biggest possible gross (before-tax) signing bonus.

But they are only focused on the sticker price -- not how much you'll have left after taxes.

In determining a professional's primary role, a good rule of thumb is to follow the money. How are they compensated?

Your agent has specialized expertise and has accomplished their goal once they secure your contract. An agent is paid a percentage based on your contract's gross (before tax) value.

This motivates your agent to negotiate the highest possible bonus and salary. In this instance, both of your interests are aligned, which is a win-win situation for both parties.

However, once the gross amount has been negotiated, an agent's vested financial interest disappears. What you choose to do with your money has no financial impact on your agent.

This is NOT a criticism against agents. Instead, it emphasizes the importance of hiring financial experts to perform jobs where their interests align with yours.

As a player, your ultimate goal is not the gross (before-tax) amount you earn; it is the net (after-tax) amount. Therefore, it is critical for a player to leverage the expertise of not only an agent but also a Certified Public Accountant (CPA) and a Certified Financial Planner (CFP®). All of them must specialize in working with professional athletes.

In fact, the best agents consult with athlete wealth management firms like ours all the time to make sure their clients have qualified advisors in place.

Ultimately, it's your responsibility to make sure the after-tax planning for your signing bonus has been considered.

One of the best ways to do that is to be proactive. Don't wait until draft day, then ask your agent, "What will we do about the taxes?"

Next thing you know, the agent responds, "Oh, I've asked, but the club won't negotiate."

Bad move.

Please make sure you hire a qualified financial team. Do this well in advance of the draft.

Make sure everyone is on the same page and they understand their roles.

Set up meetings between your agent and your financial team. Monitor it. Guide it.

Remember, you are the CEO of your life and your career.

WHAT CONVERSATIONS SHOULD I HAVE WITH MY AGENTS THROUGH THIS PROCESS?

Your agent should have no issue working with an independent financial team.

You're paying them a significant portion of your signing bonus (typically $50,000 per every $1 million you will earn), and they work for you.

But for tax planning, you need specialized expertise. Your agent can only do so much. That's why I keep reiterating the importance of having a team of experts.

We love the saying, "Trust, but always verify."

What's the best way to verify?

Ask your agent and your financial team this question:

"Can I please see a copy of a contract from a previous draft where you negotiated the signing bonus and structured it in the most tax-efficient way?"

If your agent or financial team gives you a blank stare, consider that a red flag. Either they don't know how to help you, or they don't care enough about your long-term financial health.

WHAT DOES THE CONTRACT SAY ABOUT YOUR BONUS?

Once you sign, you're bound by every word on your contract.

You'll be facing pressure to sign and close a deal quickly, but it's essential to review every detail of that contract carefully.

Many assume that the fine print is just throwaway text as if it's just the extra wrapping on a birthday present. But the fine print may have crucial information. Not just about your signing bonus but also other vital details that could affect your career and personal life.

It's always good to have an attorney review your contract.

However, it's equally important to consult with wealth advisors who understand the tax implications of the payment structure, including a CFP® and CPA.

A few key details in your contract affect how your signing bonus is taxed. Check if it has any clauses that will affect your payments' timing, structure, conditions, and amount.

For example, the standard Minor League Uniform Contract has a "Recoupment Special Covenant Clause" that can dramatically impact how much tax you pay on the bonus.

According to the IRS, a bonus can't be conditional on playing games for the team, and it can't be refundable.

Under this clause, the player forfeits the bonus if there's an unexcused absence lasting two weeks or more during any required training or during the season (regular season or post-season). The player also has to refund the bonus to the club if certain conditions are not met.

That means the IRS taxes the payments as regular wages,

subject to **state taxes where you played through the season.**

This is known as the allocation of wages according to duty days.

A true signing bonus would be **subject to state taxes where you reside**.

Depending on your state of residence and where you play, this distinction could mean the difference between paying no state income tax -- and paying hundreds of thousands of dollars.

This standard clause proves that it's essential to read every word of your contract. And that includes the fine print, even if you have to hold a magnifying glass to it.

HOW MUCH ARE SIGNING BONUSES TAXED?

A signing bonus may seem fantastic at face value. But when you consider its worth after taxes, it may amount to significantly less money.

Your taxes can vary greatly depending on several factors:

- The language of your contract

- The timing of payment

- Your residency (state taxes)

All of these factors come into play when determining your tax liability. No two cases are the same, and it's essential to get individualized advice for your situation.

Let's discuss each factor.

LANGUAGE OF YOUR CONTRACT

Unfortunately, the Standard Minor League Uniform Contract contains an "Abandonment Clause," which makes income apportioned part of your regular wages under this clause. In simple terms, your signing bonus is taxed in the state(s) in which you play.

The Abandonment Clause States:

"If player fails to report for, or abandons Club without permission and is absent from Club for a material portion, or for at least two weeks, of any playing season (which includes the championship season, any training required by Club in preparation for such championship season and any post-season that the team or affiliate to which Player is assigned participates) during the term of this Minor League Uniform Player Contract ("UPC"),

- Player shall relinquish and forfeit any right to, and Club shall not be obligated to pay, any portion of the amount not yet paid pursuant to the payment schedule set forth in this signing provision and

- Player shall immediately return and refund to the Club, and relinquish and forfeit any right to, that portion of the signing bonus already paid to Player by Club, regardless of the year of payment, that exceeds the amount of signing bonus already paid to Player by Club (i) multiplied by the number of championship seasons Player reported to, and did not subsequently abandon without permission, Club and (ii) divided by the number of championship seasons covered by the team of this UPC."

The addition of this language to the contract violates the following two conditions of a true "signing" bonus, resulting in the income being apportioned as part of regular wages:

1. the bonus is not conditional on playing any games for the team; and

2. is not refundable.

As a simple illustration, take the following two scenarios:

	True Bonus	Regular Wages
Signing Bonus	$1,000,000	$1,000,000
Team	Miami Marlins	Miami Marlins
Resident State	Texas	Texas
Team Assignment	NY	NY
Team State Tax	8.5%	8.5%
State Tax	$ 0	$ 85,000

As you can see, the impact of whether a player's signing bonus is considered a true "signing bonus" versus regular wages carries significant tax consequences. This is one of the many factors you must consider when negotiating your signing bonus. However, this is also the most difficult to change.

TIMING OF PAYMENTS

As a result of COVID-19, the typical bonus payment structure of two installments over two calendar years was eliminated for the 2020 & 2021 MLB Draft, eliminating a player's ability to maximize their after-tax signing bonus through uneven payment splits.

Thankfully, the new 2022 Collective Bargaining Agreement reinstituted the historical structure.

Players will now be able to maximize their after-tax dollars through optimizing the graduated Federal Tax Brackets and allocation of wages to states with smaller tax liabilities.

Here's an example of how much a draftee can save in taxes by correctly timing payments to make this concept tangible.

In both scenarios, the draftee received a $4,500,000 signing bonus.

Scenario A: Common Approach

$4,500,000 signing bonus = $2,597,100 net after tax

This is a fictional scenario, but it's the most common approach. The player receives half of the bonus money upfront and the other half the following year.

In this scenario, the player would have received a gross amount of $2,250,000 in year one, then the second payment for $2,250,000 in year two.

This would have resulted in an after-tax amount of $2,597,100.

Unfortunately, that's the arrangement that the player allowed his agent and team to structure.

If he had consulted with a qualified CPA before agreeing to the standard timing of payments, he could have saved more than $100,000 in taxes.

Scenario B: Tax Planning Approach:

$4,500,000 signing bonus = $2,712,900 net after tax

This scenario is based on a real draftee who worked closely with our group and his agent before signing the contract. Together, we structured the signing bonus in the most tax-efficient way possible.

The result?

$115,800 in after-tax savings

Here's how we did it.

An efficient payment structure for this draftee consisted of two uneven payments:

$4,000,000 in year one and $500,000 in year two.

Combined with *three* additional tax planning strategies, the result was a total net compensation of $2,712,900.

Compared to the draftee from Scenario A, our client had a tax savings of $115,800.

That's why working with an experienced financial team is so crucial.

RESIDENCY AND STATE TAXES

Where you live can dramatically affect your signing bonus tax rate. Income tax rates vary by state, with a handful of states currently having no income tax. There are also many localities and cities that have also implemented income taxes.

Professional athletes are subject to taxation in each jurisdiction in which they perform services (play games), making residency selection a critical planning tool.

Only eight states are free of personal income tax:

- Alaska

- Nevada

- Florida

- Texas

- Tennessee

- Washington

- South Dakota

- Wyoming

So, as a professional athlete, if you live in one of these states, you'll save a lot of money on taxes.

On the other end of the spectrum is California, the state with the highest personal income tax rate at 13.3%.

The team will typically withhold state taxes in the state where the player is assigned. In cases where the team state is a "no income tax" state, the team will not withhold any state tax, which could result in surprise and lost deductions when the resident return is filed.

State taxes need to be considered for your resident state and the states you play in during the season. Both need to be planned to maximize the benefit and reduce your tax liability.

State residency is one of the hottest topics among professional athletes, but it's also one of the most misunderstood. The days are over of simply using someone else's address and getting a new driver's license as a way to "claim" residency. States have become savvier and are proactive in securing what they believe is their rightful claim of an athlete's income.

You should consider these things as you select your place of residence. And remember, language in your contract can impact state taxes too. **According to the IRS, if it's not a true bonus, you'll pay income tax in the state where you play -- not where you reside.**

CAPTURE EVERY DOLLAR OWED

Now you have the answers to how signing bonuses are taxed.

That's great. Because the last thing you want to do is leave thousands of dollars on the table.

The bottom line is that you need a plan to lower your taxes long before you receive your signing bonus when you have a chance to negotiate and plan for the best possible contract.

Below is a sample of the type of tax projection you should be presented before you sign your contract to understand the planning for negotiating your after-tax signing bonus.

AWM Capital

	Scenario 1	Scenario 2	Scenario 3	Scenario 4
Year 1				
Signing Bonus	1,750,000	3,500,000	3,000,000	3,300,000
Regular Wages	4,500	4,500	4,500	4,500
Endorsement Income (estimated)	10,000	10,000	10,000	10,000
Less Retirement Plan Contribution	(10,000)	(10,000)	(10,000)	(10,000)
Less Standard Deduction	(12,000)	(12,000)	(12,000)	(12,000)
Less Qualified Business Income Deduction	-	-	-	-
Taxable Income	1,742,500	3,492,500	2,992,500	3,292,500
Federal tax liability (estimated)	611,000	1,259,000	1,073,000	1,185,000
State tax liability (estimated)				
Social Security	7,979	7,979	7,979	7,979
Medicare	39,431	80,556	68,806	75,856
Year 1 - Total tax liability (estimated)	658,410	1,347,535	1,149,785	1,268,835
Year 1 - Estimated cash (net of Federal and state taxes)	1,091,590	2,152,465	1,850,215	2,031,165
Year 2				
Signing Bonus	1,750,000	-	500,000	200,000
Regular Wages	9,000	9,000	9,000	9,000
Endorsement Income (estimated)	10,000	10,000	10,000	10,000
Less Retirement Plan Contribution	(10,000)	-	(10,000)	(10,000)
Less Standard Deduction	(12,000)	(12,000)	(12,000)	(12,000)
Less Qualified Business Income Deduction	-	-	-	-
Taxable Income	1,747,000	7,000	497,000	197,000
Federal tax liability (estimated)	612,500	1,500	150,000	45,000
State tax liability (estimated)	104,800	400	29,800	11,800
Social Security	7,979	558	7,979	7,979
Medicare	39,537	131	10,162	3,112
Year 2 - Total tax liability (estimated)	764,816	2,589	197,941	67,891
Year 2 - Estimated cash (net of Federal and state taxes)	985,184	(2,589)	302,059	132,109
Total estimated cash (net of Federal and state taxes)	2,076,800	2,149,900	2,152,300	2,163,300
Estimated Tax Savings		73,100	75,500	86,500

AWM Capital

4

ESTABLISHING RESIDENCY

How High Are Individual Income Tax Rates in Your State?

Top State Marginal Individual Income Tax Rates, 2021

Note: Map shows top marginal rates: the maximum statutory rate in each state. This map does not show effective marginal tax rates, which would include the effects of phase-outs of various tax preferences. Local income taxes are not included.
(*) State has a flat income tax.
(**) State only taxes interest and dividends income.
Sources: Tax Foundation; state tax statutes, forms, and instructions; Bloomberg BNA

Where you live can have a dramatic effect on your overall tax situation. Income tax rates vary by state, with a handful of states currently having no income tax. Currently, there are also many localities and cities that have also implemented income taxes. Professional athletes are subject to taxation in each jurisdiction in which they perform services, making residency selection an important planning tool.

The team will typically withhold state taxes in the state where the player is assigned. In cases where the team state is a "no income tax" state, the team will not withhold any state tax, which could result in surprise and lost deductions when the resident return is filed. State taxes need to be considered for your resident state and the state or states you play in during the season. Both need to be planned to maximize the benefit and reduce your overall tax liability.

How big of a business is it for a state?

The LA Times states that California raked in $102 million in taxes from visiting athletes in 2006-07, the last year for which records are available. "States are focusing their resources on where they can get the money," says Joseph Henchman, tax counsel and director of state projects for the Tax Foundation, an educational group based in Washington D.C.

For example, last October, it was reported that California is still pursuing a 2002 1st round pick[2] for tax, penalty, and interest totaling $433,121 over a residency dispute.

HOW TO ESTABLISH RESIDENCY

Once you decide where you want to live and start setting up your home base, you will need to do several things to ensure that you are considered a resident there. States are auditing professional athletes more and more for trying to avoid state tax. If you are going to establish residency in a new state, these steps will help you do it right and justify your case if you are audited.

The first step in the process is to establish that you are a resident of the new state. Through our experience, we have

---

[2] Out of respect, we have chosen to keep this player's name confidential.

found that the following steps help the most when audited by a state:

1. Driver's License in new state

2. Register car in new state

3. Documentation to substantiate where you live in new state:

   - Rental/lease agreement

   - Home Purchase closing statement

   - Utility Bills

   - Renter's/Homeowner's Insurance

   - Bank Statements with new address

4. Bank statements showing when earnings were received. If you move in April, earnings from February could go towards original state.

5. Copies of credit card statements to show transaction locations in off weeks (Yes, they can and will subpoena these).

6. Copies of bank/debit card statements. They will be analyzed like your credit card statements.

Once you have established yourself as "residing" in the new state, the next important factor in justifying residency is going to come down to how much time you spend in each state. I have heard many different rumors/myths/wrong information/bad advice circulating through the years when it comes to this.

Having gone through state audits with clients, here are the facts:

Two main calculations will be considered when it comes to how much time you spend in each state.

First, if you spend 183 days or more in a particular state, that state can require you to pay state income tax. So, if you are trying to NOT reside in California, you need to make sure that you spend less than 183 days in California, whether for work or not.

Second, where are you staying when you are not on the road? There is no rule about how much time you need to spend where, but you need to show that you are residing in your new state. Let's use the example of moving from California to Nevada. If you only spend an occasional few days in Nevada and spend most of your off time in California, even if you stay under the 183-day rule, you will have difficulty justifying that you are a resident of the new state. This is why going through the above steps to establish your home base is crucial.

You can insert any two states in there that apply to you. Essentially you will need to do two things: (1) establish that you are a resident of the new state, and (2) prove you did not spend over half the year in your old state.

When establishing residency in a new state, it is essential to be proactive with your record keeping. Keep track of when you moved with a rental agreement or record of purchasing your new home. Keep bank statements showing the transactions in the new state. Keep track of what days you are where for that first two years so that you don't have to go back and try to figure it out. An audit likely will not happen for a couple of years, as most state tax agencies are behind a few years. Keeping track of these details in real-time makes the audit process much smoother.

We have gone through state residence audits with multiple clients over the years. Some are straightforward and just require providing clarification on off-weeks and some administrative hurdles. For others, it can be more in-depth.

For a high-profile client, the state of NY wanted to classify him as a resident, even though he genuinely was a resident of Florida. All of the steps had been taken to establish residency in Florida, and documentation was provided. The state of NY even subpoenaed his phone records to determine his location each day of the year and credit card and bank statements to see where spending took place each day of the year. This was legal for them to request, and he had to comply, ultimately proving that he was not a resident of New York and was, in fact, a resident of Florida. The tax bill difference would have been multiple millions of dollars.

Ultimately, you need to consider many things when deciding where to live. Some will be tax-related, some will be baseball-related, and some will be family and lifestyle-related. What is suitable for one player will differ from another. Use all these considerations when making the best decision for you.

5

MANAGING YOUR BUSINESS

Financial planning is essential to everyone, but for a professional athlete, several statistics highlight that it is more critical for you to understand the fundamentals of proper financial management.

PROFESSIONAL ATHLETES

- 4.8 years is the average career length for an MLB pitcher.
- 5.6 years is the average career length for an MLB position player
- 90% of their lifetime income before the age of 35
- Are required to pay income taxes in every state they play
- Have unpredictable careers and often a lack of education qualifications

From this data, it becomes apparent that understanding the basics of financial planning as an athlete is essential to making sure that your money lasts and continues to grow.

KEY POINTS

- Your money may need to last longer than you expect.

- You have fewer working years to build up your savings and more retirement years to spend it, which increases the risk of running out of money.

- Over a long retirement, even 3% inflation can cut your purchasing power almost in half over 20 years.

- It's your younger self's job to look after your older self.

It is hard to be concerned about what will happen 20 to 30 years in the future while you are focused on performing at the highest level on the field today.

Especially when you have just started your career!

However, it's the best time because you can still do something about it. The overarching goal for most players is to have enough money at the end of their career that allows them to transition into the next phase of life without any lifestyle change. This will enable you to do what you want to do rather than what you have to do.

AM I SET FOR LIFE?

As a general rule, you will need 30 - 35 times that amount in income-producing investments for every dollar of annual spending. If your goal is to spend $100,000 per year, you need $3 million to secure this lifestyle without spending your principal when you retire from baseball.

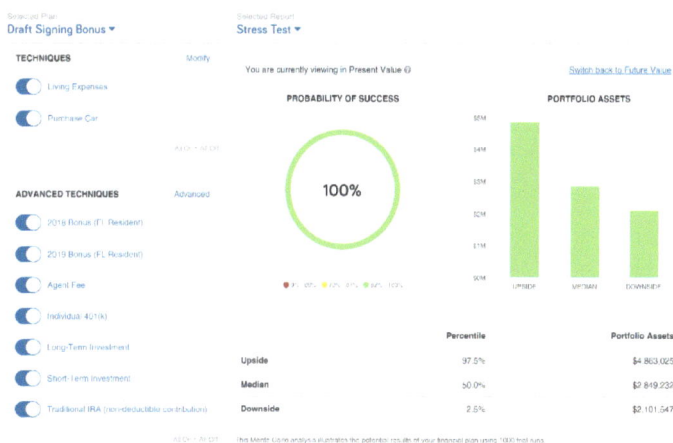

When working with potential draftees, we spend a lot of time educating the player on what a potential signing bonus actually "buys" them long-term. For most players, simply telling them they need to be careful with their money doesn't work. **Trying to convince a player who just signed for $3 million that he could run out of money quickly is not easy.**

Put yourself in the player's shoes; what's an extra pair of Jordan's, or why not spend $80,000 on a new Ford Raptor?

These are real questions that we help our clients work through. We make abundantly clear that our job is not to try and "control" our client's money; rather, our job is to teach our clients how to make great financial decisions. We reiterate that this is your money, and we want to make sure you spend your money on what is most important to you.

Purchasing a car is usually the first opportunity to help players work through a big purchase and what it means long-term from a financial perspective.

This is a great time to introduce the rule of 72.

RULE OF 72

The rule of 72 is a shortcut to estimating the number of years required to double your money at a given annual rate of return.

Years required to double investment = 72 ÷ compound annual interest rate

Using a 7.2% annualized rate of return, a player's investment balance would double every ten years.

With the Rule of 72, it's easier to see the difference between buying a new $80,000 Ford Raptor versus a $50,000 used Ford Raptor. It's not just $30,000, but the value of that money plus interest throughout your life.

If a player is 18, their investment accounts have the potential to approximately double five times before the average retirement age of 65.

So, the $30,000 difference is potentially a $960,000 decision.

- $60,000 at age 28

- $120,000 at age 38

- $240,000 at age 48

- $480,000 at age 58

- $960,000 at age 68

These are just hypothetical numbers and based on the various investment return assumptions, but this is also a very relatable scenario to help start understanding the long-term effects of the decisions you make with your money today. With this information, you can now decide if making the car purchase today is worth forgoing the potential money in the future.

YOU NEED A PLAN (AKA BUDGET)

We are often asked what the "right" amount of money to sign for is. Our first response is that the amount doesn't matter if a player doesn't have a plan in place. Even the first pick overall will run out of money without a plan in place.

For example, review the following two charts that show how quickly expenses can add up.

$2,325,250 Signing Bonus Example

Year 1

Signing Bonus	1,500,250
Regular Wages	4,500
Endorsement Income (estimated)	10,000
Less: Retirement Plan Contribution	(9,850)
Less: Agent Fees	-
Less: tax liability (estimated)	(634,816)
Net Income	**865,434**

Year 2

Signing Bonus	825,000
Regular Wages	9,000
Endorsement Income (estimated)	10,000
Less: Retirement Plan Contribution	(9,850)
Less: Agent Fees	(93,010)
Less: tax liability (estimated)	(311,053)
Net Income	**513,947**
Total estimated cash (net of taxes & agent fees)	**1,286,400**
Less: Auto Purchase	50,000
Less: 5 Years of Annual Expenses (Table 2)	150,000
Estimated cash after 5 years	1,086,400

Category	Monthly Amount	
	In-Season	**Off-Season**
Shopping	100	300
Discretionary	250	500
Food	500	500
Auto Insurance	300	300
Fuel	150	250
Mortgage/Rent	300	-
Renter's Insurance	25	25
Utilities	100	
Cell Phone	100	100
Dental Insurance	10	10
Umbrella Insurance	75	75
Clubhouse Dues	100	
Training Costs		500
Total Annual Expenses		**29,820**

MINOR LEAGUE SALARY STRUCTURE

The 2022 MLB CBA sets minimum salaries for players on 40-man rosters, with a significant increase for players under their second major league contract or with at least one day of major league service time. Free agent players can negotiate higher salaries.

40 Man Minimum Salary

Year	1st year players	2nd year +
2022	$57,200	$114,100
2023	$58,800	$117,400
2024	$60,300	$120,600
2025	$62,000	$123,900
2026	$63,600	$127,100

The CBA does not cover players who are not on 40-man rosters and have no major league service time. In fact, they are excluded from federal minimum wage laws. They are not paid for spring training or the extra hours they put in. In 2022, MLB has ordered teams to provide housing.

Here is their minimum pay scale.

Minor League Salaries

Level	Minimum pay	23 weeks
Rookie	$400/week	$9,200
Hi A, Low A	$500/week	$11,500
AA	$600/week	$13,800
AAA	$700/week	$16,100

A WORKOUT PLAN FOR YOUR MONEY

The best analogy we use to communicate the importance of a budget is to relate it to using a workout program. If you have a goal to gain ten pounds of muscle, a good strength coach will put together a program with the proper exercises that, combined with the right diet, will help you achieve your goal. The caveat is that you have to actually follow the program.

Like a workout program and diet, a budget is no different. We work with our clients to define what success means to them and then help them construct a spending plan to achieve it.

Another mistake we often see is doing the work upfront to create a budget but not reviewing it regularly. A team can only evaluate if a player is good through statistical analysis. The same holds for your money. We provide our clients with real-time tracking of their spending and financial plan so they know exactly where they are and if any adjustments need to be made. You have worked hard for this money, don't leave it to chance.

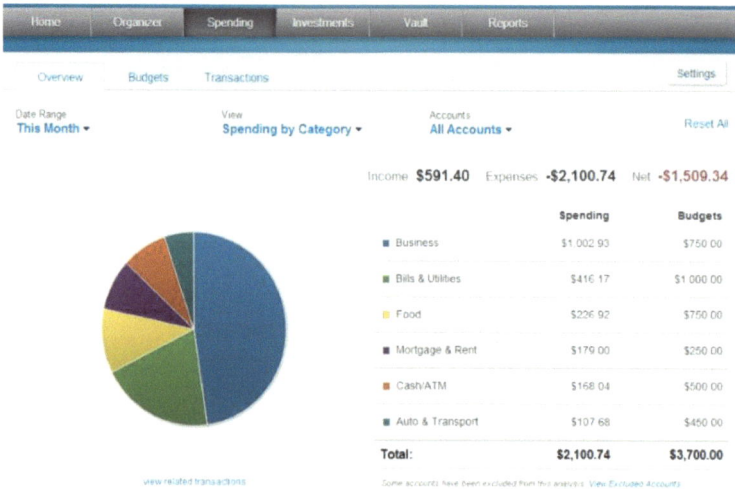

Home	Organizer	Spending	Investments	Vault	Reports

| Overview | Budgets | Transactions | | | Settings |

Date Range	View	Accounts		
This Month ▼	Spending by Category ▼	All Accounts ▼		Reset All

Income **$591.40**   Expenses **-$2,100.74**   Net **-$1,509.34**

	Spending	Budgets
■ Business	$1,002.93	$750.00
■ Bills & Utilities	$416.17	$1,000.00
■ Food	$226.92	$750.00
■ Mortgage & Rent	$179.00	$250.00
■ Cash/ATM	$168.04	$500.00
■ Auto & Transport	$107.68	$450.00
Total:	**$2,100.74**	**$3,700.00**

view related transactions

Some accounts have been excluded from this analysis. View Excluded Accounts

6

THE FINANCIAL ADVICE YOU NEED

Before we jump into **who** you should hire, we need to know **what** you are hiring them to do.

What do you think about when you hear financial advice or financial advisor?

Investments?

That is because most companies and individuals who refer to themselves as financial advisors only provide limited investment advice.

True financial advice is not solely investment advice.

Investments are critically important; however, it is only one component of making wise decisions.

An analogy that may be helpful is to think about investments as a car's engine. Incredibly powerful; however, it's not the actual car. There is a body frame, wheels, windows, a steering wheel, seatbelts, and many more features. Many components make up a high-performance vehicle. In addition, the car is a means to an end. The purpose of the vehicle is to take you from where you are Today to the desired destination.

"Financial advice" is about more than just managing an investment portfolio; it touches every aspect of your life and career.

REAL ADVICE: MAXIMIZING YOUR NET-WORTH

On any given day, you can find professional athletes training with the best strength coaches in the world. Yet, as an athlete, your goal is not to become a world-class weightlifter. You lift weights in a specialized way to help you become elite at your specific position on the field. You are a baseball player, not a weightlifter. The weights are a means to an end.

The same principle applies to money.

Money is a tool to pay for what's important to you and impact the people and causes you care about.

Investments, like weights, are a means to the end.

The outcome you want to optimize for is maximizing your Net Worth to pay for what's important. Ideally, forever without having to work. That's success.

To achieve this requires a team of experts across tax, investment, insurance, legal, and business. Yet, most advisors only provide investment advice on a limited amount of your money.

Expert financial advice begins with making sure you will receive the most money after-tax.

TAXES: #1 DESTROYER OF WEALTH

It's not what you make; it's what you keep. Taxes are the number one destroyer of wealth.

As a professional athlete who will be in the highest tax bracket, 40 to 50% of every dollar may be destroyed by taxes. Wealthy people know that a dollar saved is more valuable than a dollar earned. In this case, It's the equivalent of making 40 to 50%, which is nearly impossible to do in investing.

Starting with federal income tax, only 1% of the population will earn enough to be subject to the highest marginal federal income tax bracket. For single-filers, the 2021 Federal Income Tax Brackets are as follows:

Tax rate	Taxable income bracket	Tax owed
10%	$0 to $9,950	10% of taxable income
12%	$9,951 to $40,525	$995 plus 12% of the amount over $9,950
22%	$40,526 to $86,375	$4,664 plus 22% of the amount over $40,525
24%	$86,376 to $164,925	$14,751 plus 24% of the amount over $86,375
32%	$164,926 to $209,425	$33,603 plus 32% of the amount over $164,925
35%	$209,426 to $523,600	$47,843 plus 35% of the amount over $209,425
37%	$523,601 or more	$157,804.25 plus 37% of the amount over $523,600

MULTI-STATE TAXATION

While the average individual only pays taxes in their resident state, you as an athlete file taxes in your home state and every state—and some cities—in which you play. Because players come from all over and move around so often, many teams will report income and withhold taxes in every state you play, regardless of whether a reciprocity agreement with your home state is in place. If your tax professional understands reciprocity agreements and how to utilize them, you can save thousands of dollars a year.

Due to the lower tax rates and the sources of income described next, income tax planning is not a significant concern for the average individual because they pay a small percentage of their income to taxes. The opposite is true for professional athletes, as they are in a higher tax bracket and are subject to multiple state and local income taxes every year.

SOURCES OF INCOME

Another tax consideration is the different sources of income that you receive as an athlete. Typically, the average individual only receives "W-2 wages," and taxes are automatically withheld from their paychecks. While this is convenient, there is little opportunity for significant tax planning.

As an athlete, in addition to the W-2 wages from your team, you can earn off-the-field income that is considered 1099 miscellaneous income. With 1099 income, taxes are not automatically withheld, which provides opportunities to utilize advanced tax planning strategies.

INVESTMENT STRATEGIES

The third significant difference is your tax situation's impact on your investment returns. As stated above, only 1% of individuals are subject to the highest tax rates. Therefore, most investment options and strategies do not consider taxes when purchasing. As an affluent athlete, after-tax returns are the only returns that matter for taxable accounts because dividend and realized capital gains distributions are subject to state, local, and federal taxation. **Ignoring the impact of taxes on your investment returns is one of the biggest mistakes.**

Unfortunately, this is where most traditional financial advice completely breaks down. If you were to look at the disclosures on the bottom of the website of big Wall Street names, Merrill Lynch, Morgan Stanley, UBS, and Wells Fargo, you would see the statement, "We do not provide tax advice. All decisions regarding the tax implications of your investments should be made in consultation with your independent tax advisor."

What is arguably the most important component of financial advice is wholly ignored. **Wall Street "sells" you on comprehensive advice, but their disclosures tell the truth.**

These companies do not provide comprehensive financial advice; they sell limited investment products that they try to scale across as many people as possible.

As a professional athlete, you require integrated financial advice across your income, investments, and business decisions every day.

What About Checks & Balances?

A common rebuttal to why an advisor does not offer tax advice is checks and balances. We believe 100% in having checks and balances, but that is not accomplished by separating your tax CPA. Interview any tax CPA and ask them what information on a client's tax return would inform them of what decisions are made with your spending and investments. Their answer would be almost nothing.

There is a difference between tax preparation and financial auditing. These are two different services and are offered by different specialists.

We encourage our clients to hire the following specialists for checks and balances.

1. CPA Auditor

2. Certified Fraud Examiner

3. Attorney

The Truth Of Why Wall Street Doesn't Provide Tax Advice

The Wall Street business model is to gather as many investment assets across as many people as possible. As you read previously, it is not to provide comprehensive advice.

According to Forbes, the largest brokerage firm, Morgan Stanley has approximately 16,000 financial advisors with an average of 200 clients per advisor. That is 3,200,000 clients! The average account size of a client is $425,000. And that is only one company.

- Only 0.1% of single people or 0.7% of married couples are in the highest tax bracket.

- 80% of individuals pay less than 15% in taxes.

As you can see, most of Wall Street's clients are mass affluent and pay a lower effective tax rate than the capital gains rate of 20%. Tax planning is irrelevant for most of their clients.

The Wall Street model is not built for you.

Significant tax savings will be missed if your team does not have a qualified CPA on staff.

ATHLETES & MONEY: YOU ARE DIFFERENT THAN EVERYONE ELSE

You have heard it said before that you are different from the average individual regarding wealth, but how exactly? The apparent financial difference is that your signing bonus and salary as an athlete are far greater than the average individual, but that is only the beginning. As an athlete, you face many financial and legal challenges that the average individual will never encounter. These include but are not limited to multi-state taxation, significant asset protection concerns arising from your high liability as a public figure, complex estate tax planning, and investment concerns.

Earnings Cycle vs. Lifestyle Spending

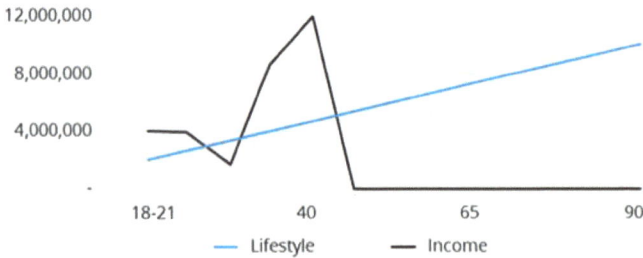

UNDERSTANDING YOUR AFFLUENCE

The first difference between you and the average individual is income level. In 2021, the national median family income for the United States was $79,900, according to the U.S. Census Bureau. In 2021, the average MLB player salary was $4.17 million, and the new MLB minimum is $700,000.

HOW DO ATHLETES MEASURE UP AMONGST AMERICA'S WEALTHY?

As an MLB player, there is a 75% likelihood of earning $10 million in your career. There is a 53% likelihood you will earn $25 million. And finally, there is a 38% likelihood you will earn $50 million or more in your career.

The average individual earns just enough to pay the bills, and very few share the same wealth level.

- **4%** of Americans have a net worth of $1 million+

- **.5%** of Americans have a net worth of $5 million+

- **0.05%** of Americans have a net worth of $25 million+

Source: CNN Money

EARNINGS CYCLE

In addition to the vast difference in the level of income is when you will earn your income throughout your lifetime.

The average individual…

- will work 35 to 45 years

- will enjoy peak earnings during the five years before retirement

The average professional athlete…

- 4.8 years is the average career of an MLB pitcher

- 5.6 years is the average career for an MLB position player

- You will likely earn 70% to 90% of your lifetime earnings before age 40

ASSET PROTECTION

In addition to estate tax planning, asset protection is a consideration that is only a concern for professional athletes, celebrities, and the wealthy. Asset protection, the practice of shielding wealth from potential lawsuits, creditors, or other claims, is not of interest to the average American because:

- They do not have significant assets to protect

- They do not face substantial liability as a public figure or through their investments

ESTATE TAX PLANNING

Under Today's laws, the estate and gift tax exemption is $12.06 million per individual. That means an individual can leave $12.06 million to heirs and pay no federal estate or gift tax. A married couple will be able to shield $24.12 million from federal estate and gift taxes. As a result, the importance of reducing estate tax liabilities is not likely to be a significant concern of the average individual.

EMBRACING YOUR UNIQUENESS

As you are likely starting to understand, you are very different from the average individual in so many ways as an athlete. As a professional athlete, you face specific "issues" that affect how you and your family approach life, your career, and outside ventures, which create unique possibilities that require specialized expertise and an intimate understanding of your respective world to achieve the results that you desire.

Unfortunately, most personal finance and investing information is created for the average individual earning between $35,000 and $75,000 per year, not a professional athlete. Think Dave Ramsey, Suzie Orman, and Jim Cramer. The same advice widely accepted and beneficial for the average person is often detrimental to someone in your position.

Today, there is practically an infinite number of places one can look for financial advice. However, when looking at mass media, you must understand who the target market is. The following list of news sources shows who their media kit states are their target audience:

- Fox News ($70,929 median household income)
- CNN ($76,419 median household income)
- MSNBC ($75,588 median household income)
- Wall Street Journal. ($253,100 avg. household income)
- Forbes ($146,263 mean household income)

You understand from these figures that all of the personal-finance sources listed have an average audience household income of less than $250,000. Almost all traditional financial advice that a professional athlete can find is useless and inappropriate to their specific situation.

If you want to achieve or maintain financial success, you must be comfortable with your circumstances and do things differently. A key to achieving this success is understanding that having very different financial challenges requires different types of advisors and strategies than the average individual.

MORE WEALTH, MORE COMPLEXITY

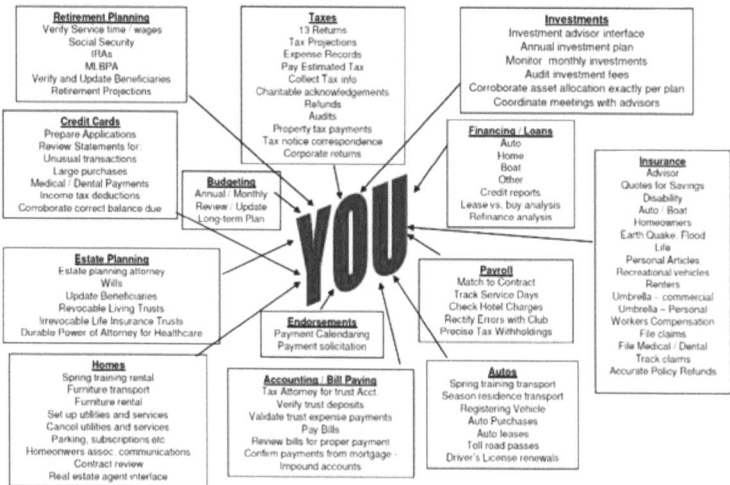

The greater the wealth of the individual or family, the more important working with a financial team becomes. There is no way one advisor could handle the needs of the super affluent. Success requires a strong team of specialized expertise.

Now that we have clarity on what services and expertise you need, we can focus on *who* **to trust.**

AWM Capital

7

WHO SHOULD YOU TRUST WITH YOUR MONEY?

There are more than 308,000 financial advisors in the United States, but very few are qualified to meet your needs. The most important investment you can make is finding the right advisory team.

That decision should be based on skill, not personality alone.

Finding qualified advisors is particularly challenging because Wall Street counts on people "buying" on personality. The industry selects, trains, and retains based on sales ability, not expertise. Accordingly, to the untrained and inexperienced eye, it is difficult to distinguish a qualified expert from one who is simply a good salesman.

> *"They hire these people not because of expertise but because they're friends. Well, they'll fail."* – Magic Johnson

It's not that likability doesn't play a role in your decision; it's just that the stakes are too high to risk your financial success on personality alone.

The cost of unqualified advice

- paying unnecessary taxes

- accepting lower returns, and

- leaving yourself exposed to higher liability

Imagine if anyone could call themselves a doctor. When hiring a doctor, you would have to try and determine, "do you know what you're doing?" We have confidence in the medical industry because there is a process that creates and demonstrates expertise and a loyalty to do no harm to a patient.

1. It takes between 10 to 14 years to become a fully licensed doctor.

    a. Four years of undergraduate studies,

    b. Eight years of medical school, and

    c. Two years of residency

2. There is a medical ethics board that holds them accountable.

3. You can trust their medication recommendations because it's illegal for doctors to receive commissions from pharmaceutical companies to push their drugs.

4. Medicine is highly specialized. It would be crazy to have an orthopedic surgeon do brain surgery!

The good news is there is a playbook for hiring qualified financial experts and avoiding the unqualified.

WHAT DO THE WEALTHIEST FAMILIES DO?

A simple and most appropriate question is, "how do the wealthiest families in the world manage their wealth?"

The answer – is they hire a team – known as a family office.

The Rockefeller family started the first family office. I'm sure you are familiar with the name, but here are a few details about the family.

John D. Rockefeller became the richest man in American history. In today's dollars, estimates of his wealth vary between $243 billion and $341 billion.

The Rockefellers had a simple mission: increasing and sustaining their family wealth across future generations. To do this, they created the first family office.

Instead of hiring multiple companies to handle different aspects of their wealth and lifestyle, they started their own. They hired a team of experts that worked solely for the family to increase and sustain their wealth across generations.

3 Pillars of a Family Office

1. **Independent:** The advice provided to the family from their staff of experts was always in the family's best interest. They could trust this was always the case because the experts they hired did not have any products to sell the family and the staff were paid only for advice. The family also knew they wanted to have the ability to invest in the best investments, not limited to what a company would sell them.

2. **Integrated:** The family knew that they had one net worth and one effective tax rate. They understood that there were no isolated decisions but that every decision impacted their net worth and taxes. The advice they needed was far beyond the capacity of any one professional advisor, therefore, they hired a well-coordinated, team of professionals from the tax, investment, insurance, estate, business and legal disciplines with years of experience.

3. **Individualized:** Lastly, they were not interested in cookie cutter options. They were not about to accept being placed into 1 of 5 options or programs that Wall Street puts 800,000 clients into. They wanted everything built specifically for them.

This is the perfect setup on how to manage your wealth.

The Rockefeller family fortune is still north of $10 billion seven generations later. More impressive is that more than 150 Rockefellers receive income from their family trusts, and they donate as much as $50 million annually.

By every definition of success, the Rockefellers have accomplished it. **The family office is the most effective and efficient way to manage your wealth.**

WHAT'S THE DIFFERENCE BETWEEN A FAMILY OFFICE AND FINANCIAL ADVISORS?

A common mistake is hiring a single "financial advisor," often from one of the large investment brokerage firms. What most of these advisors do not disclose is that you are not hiring the brainpower and resources of the firm. You have thousands of advisors working for the same company but are competitors of each other. Instead of benefiting from the collective expertise, you receive advice from one individual.

There is no way one advisor could handle the needs of the super affluent. Success requires a strong team of specialized expertise.

Family offices bring together an integrated team to align all aspects of a family's financial structure and wealth strategy. The role of the family office is to be the expert architect of a family's wealth creation. Their job is to limit roadblocks and apply their expertise to optimize the flow of money for the family. Family office advisors care about and constantly refine their craft on taxes, investments, family priorities, children, income, cash flow, liability, relationships, and legacy.

The integrated team you choose for your family office should have the proper designations and experience to manage your family's wealth professionally. If not, you're exposing yourself to unnecessary risks.

At a minimum, this integrated team of experts will consist of the following professionals:

- Certified Financial Planner (CFP®)

- Certified Public Accountant (CPA)

- Chartered Financial Analyst (CFA®)

- Certified Private Wealth Advisor (CPWA®)

- Attorney

CERTIFIED FINANCIAL PLANNER (CFP®)

The Certified Financial Planner™ (CFP®) designation is the world's most recognized personal financial planning designation. There are 85,000 CFP® professionals in the U.S. There is no reason to risk your financial future by hiring an unqualified advisor. Buyer beware.

Working with a CFP® professional is assurance that they are a credentialed expert and perform to high ethical and professional standards. The designation comes with extensive training in financial planning, estate planning, insurance, investments, taxes, employee benefits, retirement planning, and the CFP Board's Standards of Professional Conduct, which are rigorously enforced.

What It Takes To Become A CFP®

Education: The first step to CFP® certification is to acquire the knowledge required to deliver professional, competent, and ethical financial planning services to clients. CFP Board's coursework component requires the completion of a college-level program of study in personal financial planning and that every advisor has earned a bachelor's degree (or higher) from a regionally accredited college or university. Also, an advisor must complete 30 hours of continuing education (CE) accepted by the CFP Board every two years.

Examination: The CFP® Certification Examination is a two-part 6-hour exam that assesses an advisor's ability to apply their financial planning knowledge to financial planning situations in an integrated format. Combined with the education, experience, and ethics requirements, it assures the public that an advisor has met a level of competency appropriate for professional practice.

Experience: Because CFP® certification indicates an advisor's ability to provide financial planning without supervision to the public, the CFP Board requires an advisor to have 6,000 hours of experience.

Ethics: Most importantly, the CFP Board's Standards of Professional Conduct require CFP® professionals to maintain a Fiduciary Standard, which means they must look out for your interests above their own. CFP Board conducts a detailed background check for all candidates, including reviewing an advisor's involvement in any criminal, civil, governmental, or self-regulatory agency proceeding or inquiry, bankruptcy, customer complaint, filing, termination/internal reviews conducted by an employer or firm.

CERTIFIED PRIVATE WEALTH ADVISOR (CPWA®)

Certified Private Wealth Advisor ® (CPWA®) is an advanced certification for advisors to address the sophisticated needs of clients with a minimum net worth of $5 million.

High-net-worth clients have unique needs when it comes to financial planning. Many advisors consider themselves wealth managers, but only CPWA® professionals possess advanced expertise in wealth management content, strategies, and applied concepts that help better serve high-net-worth clients.

Candidates who earn the certification learn to identify and analyze challenges high-net-worth individuals **face and** understand how to develop specific strategies to minimize taxes, monetize and protect assets, maximize growth, and transfer wealth.

CPWA Qualifications

To achieve a CPWA designation, candidates must meet the prerequisite, education, and exam requirements. All candidates must obtain all the following:

Experience: A bachelor's degree from an accredited university or college or have one of the following licenses or designations: CIMA, CIMC, CFA, CFP, ChFC, or CPA license. At least five years of relevant financial services experience and a clean regulatory record

Ethics: Comply with the Institute Code of Professional Responsibility or lose the certification.

Education: Complete executive education at a top 25 global business school, including Yale School of Management or the University of Chicago Booth School of Business

Exam: Pass a rigorous five-hour examination.

Continuing competency: Stay updated on industry trends, laws, and products with 40 hours of continuing education every two years, including two hours of ethics education.

CERTIFIED PUBLIC ACCOUNTANT (CPA)

As we have discussed throughout the book, taxes are the number one destroyer of wealth. Taxes impact your income, investments, and business decisions every day.

Similar to financial advisors, hundreds of thousands of individuals prepare taxes. However, there are very few experts. Taxes are one of the most complex factors in an athlete's career. Hiring a licensed Certified Public Accountant (CPA) with specialized expertise in multi-state taxation will be a key to your success.

This is another area where we see players make bad decisions. Since nearly everyone is required to file taxes, almost everyone works with a CPA. A common mistake is assuming that all CPAs have the expertise to help athletes. Returning to the doctor analogy, you would never let any doctor perform your knee surgery. Instead, you would hire the best orthopedic surgeon that specializes in knees.

The Federal tax code is 74,608 pages long and constantly changing. It's in your best interest to hire a CPA who focuses all of their efforts on knowing how it affects you as an athlete.

If your team does not have a qualified CPA on staff, you will miss significant tax savings.

CHARTERED FINANCIAL ANALYST (CFA®)

When managing your investments, you want the best, and the CFA® charter is recognized as the most elite designation for investment professionals. The Economist magazine has called the CFA credential the "gold standard" of the investment industry.

To become a charter holder, a candidate must have four years of qualified work experience and complete the CFA Program (mastery of the current CFA curriculum and passing three six-hour examinations), which takes on average four years to complete.

ATTORNEY

Professional athletes will have various legal needs to address in their life and will need legal advice from specialists across a wide range of specific legal areas. Having a member of your family office that can help guide you through the legalese of contracts, estate planning, and investment decisions is critical. The cost of signing a document you don't fully understand can be disastrous.

If your advisory team doesn't hold these advanced designations, they have not demonstrated that they have the expertise necessary to advise you across all aspects of your wealth.

Indeed, there's a limit to what one person can accomplish. But, with access to vast resources, a team of experts has virtually no limits.

WHO NOT TO TRUST

How We Define Trust

Sadly, when you listen to interviews of people who have been victims of fraud or unqualified advice, they are shocked that it happened to them because they "trusted" that person. In the event of fraud, it was a violation of ethics. However, **in the event of unqualified advice, you may have a highly ethical advisor, but they do not have the skills or expertise to fulfill their promise.** The latter is what we experience the most. **We need a more robust definition of TRUST.**

Define Trust

In the book "The Speed of Trust" by Stephen M.R. Covey, he says, "Trust is a function of both **character** and **competence.** Character includes your integrity, your motive, and your intent with people. Competence includes your capabilities, skills, results, and track record. And both are vital."

You may trust someone's character implicitly, even enough to leave him in charge of your children when you are out of town. But you might not trust that same person in a business situation because he does not have the competence to handle it.

4 Pillars Of Trust

1. **Integrity:** You are honest and congruent, you have a reputation for being truthful, and you would not lie.

2. **Intent:** You are not trying to deceive or protect anyone, and you don't have any hidden motive or agenda.

3. **Capabilities**: That you do, indeed, have expertise, knowledge, skill, and ability in the area in which you are called to testify.

4. **Results:** You have a good track record, you have demonstrated your capabilities effectively in other situations in the past, you produced results, and there is good reason to believe that you will do so now.

As an example, I trust my dad to watch my children.

1. **Integrity:** I know my dad is honest and truthful.

2. **Intent:** His interest is wholly aligned with mine. As

their grandfather, he wants them to be healthy and well cared for.

3. **Capabilities:** He is mentally and physically able to meet the demands of watching the kids.

4. **Results:** He has a record of raising two children who are now law-abiding citizens!

However, I would never trust my dad to play quarterback for the LA Rams.

1. **Integrity:** Yes, he is honest and truthful. This alone would prevent him from lying about his ability to play quarterback in the NFL.

2. **Intent:** He may want to play quarterback, but that conflicts with what the Rams want.

3. **Capabilities**: None

4. **Results:** Proven that he cannot be trusted!

As silly as this example is, it does a great job demonstrating that genuine Trust is not character alone. **It must always be a combination of character and competence.**

Let's assume that everyone you are interviewing are people of integrity. The main focus should be spent on confirming the financial team has the intent, capabilities, and results required for you to hire them.

THE FINANCIAL PROFESSIONALS YOU SHOULD NOT TRUST

Intent: Are You Required To Do What's In My Best Interest?

If there is only one question you ask, it must be, "Do you act as a fiduciary?" What does it mean to act as a fiduciary? An advisor under the fiduciary standard is legally bound to do what's best for you in every situation.

Now, doesn't this seem like this would be the only standard? Unfortunately, it's not.

FINRA regulates brokers under what's known as the "Suitability Standard." The suitability standard is nothing less than a license to sell investors products that might not serve their best interest.

The Fiduciary Standard requires your advisor to act in your best interests. This standard, however, is governed by the Securities and Exchange Commission (SEC), not FINRA, and it only applies to advisors they have jurisdiction over.

Why Do Conflicts Of Interest Matter?

A conflict of interest is defined as a conflict between the private interests and the official responsibilities of a person in a position of trust.

If you are a Wall Street Bank/Brokerage client, you will be exposed to significant conflicts of interest. These firms are in the business of selling products and producing a profit for shareholders.

Suppose you hire someone who works for an insurance company (Mass Mutual, Prudential, i.e.) or brokerage firm (Morgan Stanley, Merrill Lynch, UBS, RBC, Wells Fargo). In that case, they are "registered representatives" and may have an incentive to sell propriety products.

This does not mean an advisor lacks integrity or is ill-willed. It just means that there is a conflict of interest.

How Can I Tell If A Person Is A Fiduciary Or A Stockbroker?

A straightforward search online to the Financial Industry Regulatory Authority (FINRA) will help you eliminate anyone who is not a Fiduciary.

1. Visit https://brokercheck.finra.org/
2. Enter the individual's name / Firm name

If you see Broker / Brokerage Firm Regulated by FINRA, they are NOT a fiduciary.

If you choose to hire a broker, you accept that the advice you receive is filled with conflict and may not be in your best interest.

The Solution: Independent Registered Investment Advisors

Thankfully for you, a whole category of advisory firms – known as registered investment advisors (RIAs) – have chosen to be bound by the more stringent fiduciary standard.

RIAs are **independent**, meaning they are not tied to any insurance products or investment products. You can have confidence that their advice is motivated by what's in your best interest, not just their profit.

You deserve advice in your best interest. Hiring an independent family office is the standard you should require.

Capabilities: Are You Qualified To Work With Someone In My Situation?

ADVICE FOR THE MASSES

Wallstreet Brokerage Firms
$425,944 average account size
221 clients per 1 adviser
14,629 financial advisors (brokers)

Limitations
Not permitted to give tax advice
Incentivized to sell you firm products
Limited investment options
Not permitted to advise on outside investments

Merrill Lynch   RBC   Morgan Stanley

WELLS FARGO   SunTrust   UBS

One of the common mistakes professional athletes make when they build out their team of advisors is to assume that **any** financial advisor is qualified to work with them.

Mainstream financial advice and **advisors** are focused on the **mass affluent** client as it represents **99% of people.**

As a professional athlete, you are now in the top 1% and require specialized advice.

Ideally, you want an advisory team with extensive experience working with people like you. Most financial advisors may be able to construct an investment portfolio. Still, not many of them specialize in working with 18- to 35-year-old individuals with sudden wealth, uneven cash flow, uncertain job security, lack of financial expertise, who are targets of lawsuits and investment scams, and who have the other complexities that come along with being a professional athlete.

When interviewing a potential financial team, the first set of questions to ask are:

1. What is the median age of your clients?

2. How many clients do you work with who are professional athletes?

3. How many of your clients have a net worth greater than $10 million?

Company Infrastructure

At a minimum, your integrated team of experts should consist of the following professionals:

- Certified Private Wealth Advisor (CPWA®)

- Certified Financial Planner (CFP®)

- Chartered Financial Analyst (CFA®)

- Certified Public Accountant (CPA)

- Attorney

RESULTS

Don't Be A Guinea Pig

If you were having heart surgery, I'm guessing you would not choose a surgeon who has only performed a few surgeries. Why would you accept anything different when it comes to your finances?

Don't let someone learn on you.

FIVE QUESTIONS TO SET THE STANDARD

With these five simple questions, you can eliminate unqualified advisors. It is that simple. If you choose to violate any of these five questions, you settle for less than the best and heed the warning, "Buyer Beware."

1. Is your company an independent Registered Investment Advisor?
   - **If no, do not pass go.**
2. Does your team include a CFP®, CPWA®, CFA®, CPA, & Attorney?
   - **If no, do not pass go.**

3. Do you provide tax advice?
   - **If no, do not pass go.**
4. Can you advise and manage a client's MLB 401(k), retirement plans, private real estate, venture capital, and private equity investments held away from your company?
   - **If no, do not pass go.**
5. Do you work with a minimum of 25 MLB players represented by at least five different agencies?
   - **If no, do not pass go.**

PEOPLE YOU TRUST IN OTHER AREAS BUT DON'T HAVE THE COMPETENCE

Your Family And Friends

Your family and friends may have been by your side supporting your career as it developed, and they may have your best interest at heart, but they may not be qualified to deal with complicated financial issues.

Besides the possible lack of experience, trusting "a friend of a friend whose cousin is an accountant" may lead to unnecessary conflicts. As soon as an athlete goes pro, people searching for handouts tend to stretch the definition of family and friends.

Coaches And Teammates

To be a successful athlete, you need to trust your coach and your teammates, but trusting them on the field does not mean they have the expertise needed when making important financial decisions. The pressure to go along with a new plan that will guarantee to make you lots of money or trust the advice of a veteran player may be strong.

Still, the desire to protect your finances and make educated decisions should be stronger for you and your family.

Your Agent
Your agent acts on your behalf in negotiating your contracts with professional teams or organizations. Some agents will also perform additional services that range from helping you supplement your income with speaking engagements or endorsements to counseling you about preparing for a career after your playing days.

It may seem like a logical fit to leave your finances in the hands of your agent, but often this is a big mistake that countless athletes have previously made.

One of the factors contributing to financial failure for many players is the evolution of one-stop shops. Agencies attempt to be "all things" – contract negotiator, marketing expert, legal advisor, wealth manager, business manager, etc., to players.

Each aspect of a player's career is complex and requires specialized knowledge, expertise, and skill. It is rare for any one company or individual to be able to provide objective expertise across all these areas. Also, the potential for conflicts of interest increases under these scenarios.

Though many well-intentioned advisors at firms suggest that they "protect" their clients from these inherent conflicts, principles can easily get compromised when doing right by the client does not maximize their compensation or their employer's profits.

An agent's primary role is to help secure the best contracts both on and off the field to compensate for the player's talent.

In determining a professional's primary role, a good rule of thumb is to follow the money. How are they paid?

Your agent has specialized expertise and has accomplished their goal once they secure your contract. An agent is paid a percentage based on your contract's gross (before tax) value. This is a motivator for your agent to negotiate the highest possible salary. In this instance, both of your interests are aligned, which is a win-win situation for both parties.

However, an agent's vested financial interest disappears once the gross amount is negotiated. What you choose to do with your money has no financial effect on your agent. This is NOT a criticism against agents but instead emphasizes the importance of hiring financial experts to perform jobs where their interests align with yours.

Your goal is not the gross (before-tax) amount you earn, but the net (after-tax) amount. Therefore, you must leverage the expertise of an agent and a Certified Public Accountant (CPA), and a Certified Financial Planner (CFP®). All of them must specialize in working with professional athletes.

YOUR AGENT & FINANCIAL TEAM SHOULD BE SEPARATE

The most effective way to be confident you are receiving objective advice in your best interest is to build a team of **independent** experts. When you build your professional team, your team is divided into separate departments with distinct and independent responsibilities and areas of expertise.

This structure ensures that no one person, department, or company has absolute control over all of your decisions. This helps protect you as each department holds the other responsible for the advice that is being provided.

The State of California feels so strongly about the importance of separation between talent representation and wealth management in the entertainment industry that they enacted specific regulations to protect consumers.

California Labor Code and California Code of Regulations, Title 8:170040:

...(b) no talent agency may refer an artist to any person, firm, or corporation in which the talent agency has a direct or indirect financial interest for other services to be rendered to the artist, including, but not limited to...business management, personal management...(c) no talent agency may accept any referral fee or similar compensation from any person, association, or corporation providing services of any type expressly outlined in subdivision (b) to an artist under contract with the talent agency.

Core Competency & Expertise

Similar to how an all-star team is chosen, you will want to select the best experts at each position.

Unfortunately, suppose your agency and wealth management are within the same company. There is a potential conflict of interest that the services being provided are not recommended because they are the best available for you, the client, but rather what produces the most revenue for the firm.

Just as you have hired an experienced agent to negotiate your contract, it is also wise to hire the most qualified team of Certified Financial Planner™ (CFP) professionals and Certified Public Accountants (CPA) with the experience and expertise of working with professional athletes.

Relationship Protection

By working with two independent firms, you can also protect your relationships from being negatively affected by one trying to advise outside their area of expertise. You do not want to fire your agent, who may be the best expert to negotiate your contract, because you are unhappy with your investment returns or vice versa.

WHAT ABOUT THE FINANCIAL GROUP MY AGENT RECOMMENDS?

This happens often and can be a great place to start your research. However, this is also one of the main culprits of players hiring incompetent and unqualified financial advisors.

Unfortunately, some agents refer to a financial advisor based on who they believe will help "protect" their relationship with the client, not who is the best-qualified expert to help their clients achieve lifelong financial success.

If an agency recommends a financial group, there are a few key questions you should ask the agency to answer as to why they are recommending a group.

- What qualifies the financial group beyond working with the agent's existing clients?

- Does the agency receive any compensation for referring their players to the financial advisor?

- Does the recommended financial group work with players represented by different agencies? This would be a good sign that the financial group is considered an expert by multiple agencies and has no "allegiances" to any one agent.

Your financial team must have a professional working relationship with your agent to help ensure all contracts are negotiated in the most tax-efficient way and align with your most important financial goals. At the same time, a clear separation between your financial team and your agency to maintain a fiduciary standard of care where no conflicts of interest will exist. Regardless of where a recommendation comes from, it is imperative to ensure you perform your due diligence and hire qualified experts.

CLOSING THOUGHTS

One last piece of advice, if we may: **Enjoy the experience!**

It is easy to become so overwhelmed with the draft process that you forget to take the time to enjoy the moment at hand.

As every former player will tell you, it doesn't last forever.

We wish you the best of success both on and off the field.

AWM Capital

8

ACTION PLAN

Before The Draft
- ✓ Determine Signability
- ✓ Signing Bonus Tax Planning Projection
- ✓ Establishing Residency Plan, if applicable
- ✓ Secure Disability Insurance, if applicable
- ✓ Bank Account Setup
- ✓ Establish Player Credit

Signing Bonus Negotiation
- ✓ Signing Bonus Tax Planning
- ✓ Contract Language
- ✓ Team Assignment
- ✓ Structure of Bonus Payout

After Signing
- ✓ W4 Filing
- ✓ Direct Deposit Setup
- ✓ In-Season Budget Planning
- ✓ Tax Planning
- ✓ Investment Planning Meeting & Implementation
- ✓ Auto Purchase, if applicable
- ✓ Auto Insurance Policy
- ✓ Off-season Budget Planning
- ✓ Personal Liability Umbrella Policy
- ✓ Estate Planning

FINANCIAL ADVISOR QUESTIONNAIRE

BACKGROUND | EDUCATION | EXPERIENCE

How long have you and your firm offered financial planning advice to professional athletes?

How many and what % of your clients are professional athletes?

What is the average age of your clients?

What financial certifications/designations/licenses do you & any advisor who will be providing advice to me hold? Visit each governing authority to verify by clicking each license or designation.

Minimum Securities License(s)?

- Series 65 or Series 66

Advanced Designation(s)?

- Certified Financial Planner™ (CFP®)
- Certified Private Wealth Advisor (CPWA®)
- Certified Public Accountant (CPA)
- Personal Financial Specialist (PFS)
- Chartered Financial Analyst (CFA®)

Are you or your firm registered as an investment adviser with the SEC or State(s)?

Have any lawsuits/allegations been levied by past or present clients relating to your work as a financial advisor or otherwise?

Verify by visiting the following:
- Securities and Exchange Commission
- Financial Industry Regulatory Authority

How much <u>professional athlete assets</u> does your firm manage?

Who holds custody of your client's funds?

Are you obligated to work with your client as a Fiduciary? Will you put that in writing?

How often can I expect to meet and speak with you as a client?

SERVICES | COMPENSATION

In addition to investment management, what other services are included in your fee?

- Budgeting? How interactive is the ongoing budgeting process?
- Insurance review and implementation?
- Real Estate consultation?
- Estate Planning consultation?
- Bill Pay?

How are you paid for your services?

- An annual percentage based on assets managed?
- Commission?
- Are there trading costs, brokerage fees, or any administrative charges?
- Tax Planning & Preparation Fee
- Bill Pay

Do you receive or send referral fees to any sports agents that refer clients to you?

INVESTMENT PHILOSOPHY

Does one individual handle my investment decisions, or is there a formalized investment committee?

Do you have a document (i.e., an investment policy statement) that clearly articulates your approach to managing your client's money?

How is your investment philosophy tax efficient?

How soon can I get access to my money if I need it?

TAX PLANNING

How often do you engage in tax planning with your clients throughout the year?

Do you have a Certified Public Accountant working for your team, or do you outsource this service?

If outsourced, how often do you consult with this expert?

How do you ensure that planning and investment decisions are made with comprehensive tax planning in mind?

As a professional baseball player, what are the most common tax planning opportunities I should be aware of?

Is your team experienced in advanced tax planning, i.e., setting up separate business structures?

TARGETED ATHLETE QUESTIONS

What are the most significant planning challenges facing your athlete clients that a non-athlete client would not face?

What do you do to help educate clients on financial planning?

AUTHORS

Erik D. Averill, CFP®, CPWA®, CKA®

Erik Averill is the co-founder of AWM. He is a CERTIFIED FINANCIAL PLANNER™ (CFP®) Professional and a Certified Private Wealth Advisor (CPWA®).

Erik had a vision and a passion for providing financial advice to professional athletes.

While most would consider the prospect of working with professional athletes as an exciting clientele, it was his experience as a former professional athlete and personal exposure to bad financial advice that fueled his desire to start AWM.

Erik was convinced that the traditional model of financial advice for athletes was broken. Athletes have made the right decision to hire a "financial advisor", however, the financial industry has failed them. The results have been disastrous.

Athletes are four times more likely to file for bankruptcy, twice as likely to be divorced, and have squandered millions due to fraud, high fees, and unqualified advice.

It was these convictions that led to the founding of AWM Capital and continue to drive the team today.

Before co-founding AWM, Erik was a professional baseball player with the Detroit Tigers and Seattle Mariners organizations. During his career as an ASU Sun Devil, Erik was a 2003 Freshman All-American Honors, 2004 & 2005 All Pacific-Ten, and Pitcher of the Year for the 2005 College World Series Team.

Personal Life

Erik is a member of Redemption Church where he serves as a Deacon. Erik lives in Tempe with his wife, Sadie and their daughter, Olivia Grace and son, Levi Patrick.

Advanced Designations & Certifications

- Certified Private Wealth Advisor (CPWA®)

- Certified Financial Planner (CFP®)

- Certified Kingdom Advisor (CKA®)

Education

- Yale School of Management – Certificate of Wealth Management Theory and Practice

- UCLA – Certificate of Personal Financial Planning

- Arizona State University – W.P. Carey School of Business, B.S. Finance

- MTC Seminary – M.A. Missional Theology

Brandon L. Averill, CFP®, CPWA®, CIPM

Brandon is the Managing Partner at AWM Capital. In 2016, Brandon was named by Investment News as one of the Top 40 Financial Advisors under age 40. Brandon loves the impact that he can have on the lives of the clients he works with and supports them in their growth, whether that's as an athlete or in building a company. Before AWM, he was a professional athlete by way of UCLA.

Before AWM, Brandon served as an assistant vice president with Union Bank's Northern California Corporate Banking team. Earlier, he was a professional athlete, having been drafted by the Houston Astros out of UCLA. While at UCLA, Brandon was the team's co-captain and graduated with a BA in Sociology and a minor in Political Science.

Brandon is a CERTIFIED FINANCIAL PLANNER™ (CFP®) professional and holds the Certificate in Investment Performance Measurement (CIPM®) from the Chartered Financial Analyst Institute (CFA).

In 2018, Brandon earned the Certified Private Wealth Advisor® certification through the University of Chicago Booth School of Business.

Brandon resides in Glendale, CA, with his wife Anne, a Chartered Financial Analyst, and three children. Brandon is passionate about wine and cycling and loves being behind the camera in his free time.

Robert D. McConchie, CPA/PFS, CKA®

Robert McConchie is a partner and co-founder at AWM Capital and has over 15 years of experience as a tax and personal financial specialist. He is a specialist in multi-state taxation and taxation of high-net-worth individuals and businesses. He was a 2018 recipient of the AICPA 'Standing Ovation' award, which recognizes young CPAs under the age of 40

Robert is the Director of the Tax Division at AWM. As a specialist in multi-state taxation, tax consulting, and tax compliance issues, he is responsible for providing expert tax advice on high-level technical issues, IRS engagements, and all areas of management of the firm.

Before joining AWM, he served as Tax Manager in the Phoenix office of Grant Thornton, one of the top 5 international accounting firms. Robert is licensed as a Certified Public Accountant (CPA®) in the state of Arizona and California and holds the Personal Financial Specialist (PFS®) credential.

Robert holds a Bachelor of Science degree in Business and Economics from Westmont College, where he was a four-year letter winner in baseball. Robert is a member of the California Society of Certified Public Accountants and the Arizona Society of Certified Public Accountants.

ABOUT AWM CAPITAL

AWM Capital's original mission was to change the culture of how and why athlete's use their wealth. Over time this mission evolved and became greater. AWM now advises multi-generational families who made their wealth as athletes and founders with integrated, individualized, and independent advice. Both athletes and founders share a similar human capital profile – i.e. much of their net worth is unrealized initially and planning ahead for future liquidity allows us to optimize a client's situation to meet their unique priorities. We now have the privilege to serve as a wealth advisor to some of the best people in sports and the business world.

The way in which we serve clients is as follows:

- **Multi-Family Office** – the most effective and comprehensive way to manage wealth.
- **Unique Clientele** – yes, the athlete is unique but what became more obvious over time was the experience that we have built-in guiding young people to steward wealth well. Very few firms have the breadth of experience that allows our team unique insight to help families transition wealth to the next generation.
- **Human Capital Approach** – recognition that a client's largest asset might be their human capital. Many times, the growth potential of a client's human capital far exceeds any growth that could be gained from a financial investment. We focus on helping our clients to maximize their human capital so that they can maximize their complete financial structure.
- **Human Centered Design** - While our industry places money at the center, our philosophy begins and ends with our families and achieving their priorities. Wealth is a tool for impact. Wealth is a

means. Not the end. Therefore, we invest heavily into our client's human capital and individualized planning.

- **Liability Matching Portfolio Construction** – most financial firms build portfolios based upon monte carlo simulations and risk tolerance questionnaires and invest in model portfolios. Rather than implement a "cookie-cutter" approach we build customized portfolios to fit our clients' priorities.